# THE LORD AND HIS PRAYER

# *The Lord and His Prayer*

## N. T. Wright

WILLIAM B. EERDMANS PUBLISHING COMPANY
GRAND RAPIDS, MICHIGAN

FORWARD MOVEMENT PUBLICATIONS
CINCINNATI, OHIO

This edition published jointly 1997
in the United States of America by
Wm. B. Eerdmans Publishing Co.
255 Jefferson Ave. S.E., Grand Rapids, Michigan 49503
and by
Forward Movement Publications
412 Sycamore Street, Cincinnati, Ohio 45202

Printed in the United States of America

01 00 99 98 97    5 4 3 2 1

Eerdmans ISBN 0-8028-4320-4
Forward Movement ISBN  0-88028-178-2

# Contents

*for Julian, Rosamund, Harriet and Oliver*

# PROLOGUE

## (i)

This book began life as a series of sermons preached in Lichfield Cathedral in Advent 1995. That explains some of its particular emphases, though I hope it will be found equally relevant wherever and whenever it is read. A few more words about its origin may help.

I have been wanting for some time to share with a different audience some of the fruits from my last ten years of academic study, working on the historical life of Jesus. I didn't want just to write another series of lectures; if my conclusions are correct, it is actually more appropriate that such thoughts should come together within the worshipping and witnessing life of the church.

Jesus' message summons us to focus our thoughts on the coming of the Kingdom of God. Because that is a huge and difficult idea, I here focus that thought, too, on one small point: namely, the prayer that Jesus taught, the so-called 'Lord's Prayer'. We live, as Jesus lived, in a world all too full of injustice, hunger, malice and evil. This prayer cries out for justice, bread, forgiveness and deliverance. If anyone thinks those are irrelevant in today's world, let them read the newspaper and think again.

The more I have studied Jesus in his historical setting, the more it has become clear to me that this prayer sums up fully and accurately, albeit in a very condensed fashion, the way in which he read and responded to the signs of the times, the way in which he understood his own vocation and mission and invited his followers to share it. This prayer, then, serves as a lens through which to see Jesus himself, and to discover something of what he was about.

When Jesus gave his disciples this prayer, he was giving them part of his own breath, his own life, his own prayer. The prayer is actually a distillation of his own sense of vocation, his own understanding of his Father's purposes. If we are truly to enter into it and make it our own, it can only be if we first understand how he set about living the Kingdom himself.

A further reason for my taking of the Lord's Prayer as my theme in the sermons from which this book developed has to do with our stated aim in the Lichfield Cathedral Strategic Plan, developed by the Chapter over the last two years. Our first priority for action, we have said, is 'to develop the prayer-life of the Cathedral.' This dovetails completely with the Lichfield Diocesan Strategic Plan, entitled 'Growing the Kingdom', in which our Bishop, Keith Sutton, has placed 'worship and prayer' as the first of our stated objectives.

One central part of our task as a Cathedral, of course, is precisely to be a powerhouse of prayer for the whole Diocese. 1995 saw the celebration of the 800th anniversary of the present (Gothic) Cathedral, built on the site of the previous Saxon and Norman ones, and we have been using our celebrations to launch various new ideas and programmes. The series of sermons which turned into this book began shortly after our celebrations had reached their climax. As we took a deep breath after all the tumult and excitement of the festivities, I couldn't think of any better way to draw 1995 towards its close than to turn our thoughts to what we all agree is one of the most central things in our life, namely, prayer.

Where better to start that than with the prayer that Jesus himself taught us? If we value and marvel at the fact that Christian worship has been offered in our

Cathedral church for nearly thirteen hundred years –
and it is indeed a wonderful thing – how much more
ought we to cherish and marvel at the fact that for
nearly two thousand years *people have prayed this
prayer.* When you take these words on your lips you
stand on hallowed ground.

(ii)

Prayer is, of course a mystery. It's become quite
commonplace to say this. Many Christians, including
many clergy, have come to accept that they don't find
prayer easy, that they don't really understand what it
does or can do. Many have become, in a puzzled sort
of way, vaguely reconciled to this perplexity, as
though it makes them in some way second-class
citizens. Some lay folk, if you ask them about their
own prayer, will tend to say 'Oh, I leave that to the
clergy.' Some clergy will say, 'Oh, I leave the
serious stuff to the monks and nuns.' Some in the
monastic communities will say 'well, we can't all be
mystics, can we?'

Well, no, I suppose not. But there is good scrip-
tural warrant for finding prayer puzzling and
mysterious. St Paul, in a famous passage, says that

'we don't know how to pray, or what to pray for, as we ought', and says that we therefore depend on God's spirit to help us, catching us up into the agonizing dialogue between the living God and the pain of the world, even though we don't really understand what's happening (Romans 8.18–27). That may be humbling, but it should also be encouraging.

Even those who have made the long journey into really serious prayer come back to tell the rest of us that it remains a great mystery, that it's often very hard work with little apparent or immediate reward. They do, however, tend then to add tantalising things about mounting up with wings like eagles, about being changed from glory into glory, about God having prepared for those who love him such good things as pass human understanding. Those people who, like Moses, disappear into the cloud of unknowing sometimes return without realising that their faces are shining.

As we pursue this mystery, then, where better to start than with the words Jesus himself taught us? The 'Lord's Prayer' has of course, like all parts of the New Testament, been subjected to rigorous historical and theological analysis. I have learnt much from this scholarly research; but this book is not the place for quoting the scholars, or noting my various discussions with them. Those who want to follow things up could read *The Prayers of Jesus* by Joachim Jeremias (SCM, 1967), though in various ways scholarship has moved on since then. There is also a good article on the Lord's Prayer by J. L. Houlden in the very useful *Anchor Bible Dictionary*. Much significant commentary on the prayer, however, is contained in the relevant section of commentaries on Matthew and Luke, and of books about Jesus himself. I refer readers to those.

How do you set about praying? From our point of view, there is a fairly obvious order of priorities. We're usually in some sort of mess, and we want God to get us out of it. Then we've usually got some fairly pressing needs, and we want God to supply them. It may strike us at that point that there's a larger world out there. Again, we probably move from mess to wants: please sort out the Middle East, please feed the hungry, please house the homeless.

But then, once more, it may dawn on us that there's not just a larger world out there; there's a larger *God* out there. He's not just a celestial cleaner-up and sorter-out of our messes and wants. He is God. He is the living God. And he is our Father. If we linger here, we may find our priorities quietly turned inside out. The contents may remain; the order will change. With that change, we move at last from paranoia to prayer; from fuss to faith.

The Lord's Prayer is designed to help us make this change: a change of priority, not a change of content. This prayer doesn't pretend that pain and hunger aren't real. Some religions say that; Jesus didn't. This prayer doesn't use the greatness and majesty of God to belittle the human plight. Some religions do that; Jesus didn't. This prayer starts by addressing God intimately and lovingly, as 'Father' – *and* by bowing before his greatness and majesty. If you can hold those two together, you're already on the way to understanding what Christianity is all about.

Before turning to the details, let me suggest three practical ways to use the Lord's Prayer, perhaps at a special time of the year such as Lent or Advent, or just as a way of developing one's prayer life.

First, there is the time-honoured method of making the Lord's Prayer the framework for regular daily praying. Take each clause at a time, and, while holding each in turn in the back of your mind, call into the front of your mind the particular things you want to pray for, as it were, under that heading. Under the clause, 'Thy Kingdom Come', for example, it would be surprising if you didn't want to include the peace of the world, with some particular instances. The important thing is to let the medicine and music of the prayer encircle the people for whom you are praying, the situations about which you are concerned, so that you see them transformed, bathed in the healing light of the Lord's love as expressed in the prayer.

Second, some people use the Lord's Prayer in the same way that some use the Orthodox Jesus-prayer. Repeat it slowly, again and again, in the rhythm of your breathing, so that it becomes, as we say, second nature. Those of us who live busy or stressful lives may find a discipline like that very difficult; but, again, it may be precisely people like that who need – perhaps, physically need – the calming and nourishing medicine of this prayer to be woven into the fabric of their subconscious. Next time you make a car journey by yourself, leave the radio switched off, and try it. Yes, it takes time. What else would you expect?

Third, you might like, for a while, to take the clauses of the prayer one by one and make each in turn your 'prayer for the day'. Sunday: Our Father. Monday: Hallowed be thy Name. Tuesday: Thy Kingdom Come. Wednesday: Give us this day. Thursday: Forgive us our trespasses. Friday: Deliver us from evil. Saturday: The Kingdom, the Power and the Glory. Use the clause of the day as your private retreat, into which you can step at any moment, through which you can pray for the people you meet, the things you're doing, all that's going on around you. The 'prayer of the day' then becomes the lens through which you see the world.

There are, of course, dozens of other ways in which this prayer can be used, by groups or by individuals. These are just some suggestions for a start. If they help any readers to discover the value of a treasure they already own, I shall be glad.

(iii)

This book is dedicated to Julian, Rosamund, Harriet and Oliver. They have put up with their father preaching sermons, taking services, writing books, travelling away from home to give lectures, and generally being busy with the things that theologians have to do but which put a strain on family life. It seems only right that they should receive a token, however small, of my love, and my gratitude for all that they are and all that they mean to me.

Tom Wright
Lichfield Cathedral

# CHAPTER ONE

# Our Father in Heaven

If we are serious at all about our Christian commitment, we will want to learn and grow in prayer. When we kneel down, or settle in the quiet chair that serves as our personal place of prayer; when we're walking along, or riding in the train to work; whenever we pray, this is what we are coming to do: to pursue the mystery, to listen and respond to the voice we thought we just heard, to follow the light which beckons round the next corner, to lay hold of the love of God which has somehow already laid hold of us.

We want all this, at our best, not because we selfishly want, as it were, to maximize our own spiritual potential. To think that way would be to import into our Christianity a very modern, materialist, self-centred ideology. No. We want it because we know, in our heart of hearts, that we want the living God. We want to know him; we want to love him. We want to be able truly to call him Father.

In a sense, therefore, the first words of the Lord's Prayer, which we examine in this first chapter, represent the goal towards which we are working, rather than the starting point from which we set out. It is no doubt true, here as elsewhere, that the end of all our striving will be to arrive where we started and know the place for the first time. But that means, I think, that, although we are given the Lord's Prayer in our baptism to be our own prayer, a special personal gift for each one of us, this prayer is not just the spiritual version of the baby's mug and spoon set, though it is surely that as well. It is the suit of clothes designed for us to wear in our full maturity. And most of us, putting the suit on week by week, have to acknowledge that it's still a bit big for us, that we still have some growing to do before it'll fit. It is true, then, that as soon as someone becomes a Christian, he or she can and must say 'Our Father'; that is one of the marks of grace, one of the first signs of faith. But it will take full Christian maturity to understand, and resonate with, what those words really mean.

In many ancient liturgies, and some modern ones, when the Lord's Prayer is said at the Eucharist, it is introduced with solemn words which recognise that to say this prayer properly, and to mean it from the heart, would imply that we had become fully, one hundred per cent, converted, Christian; that the Holy Spirit had completed the good work that God had begun in us. And, since we know that's not true, the priest says words such as these: 'As our Saviour Christ has commanded and taught us, we are bold to say. . .'. In other words, we don't yet have the right to say this prayer, but it's part of the holy boldness, the almost cheeky celebration of the sheer grace and goodness of the living God, that we can actually say these words as though we really meant them through and through. It's a bit like a child dressing up in his grown-up brother's suit, and having the cheek to impersonate him for a whole morning, and just about getting away with it; and learning to his surprise, as he does so, what it must be like to *be* that older brother.

And that, of course, is exactly what the Lord's Prayer invites us to do. The Lord's Prayer grows directly out of the life and work of the Lord himself, whom both St Paul and the author of the letter to the Hebrews describe precisely as our elder brother. We call Jesus 'the Son of God', in our hymns and creeds and prayers, and we are right to do so; but we don't often stop to think what that meant for Jesus himself. What was going on in Jesus' life when he called God 'Father', and taught his followers to do so too?

People used to say that nobody before Jesus had called God 'Father'. They also used to say that the word *Abba*, which Jesus used in the Garden of Gethsemane and quite possibly on other occasions, was the little child's word, 'Daddy', in the Hebrew or Aramaic of his day. People therefore used to say that Jesus thus introduced, and offered to the world, a new level of personal intimacy with God. This conclusion may, in some sense, be true; but the two pillars on which it stood are shaky. Plenty of people called God 'Father', in Judaism and elsewhere. And *Abba* is in fact a word with much wider use than simply on the lips of little children. So what did it mean for Jesus himself that he called God 'Father'?

The most important thing, which is really the starting-point for grasping who Jesus was and is, is that this word drew into one point *the vocation of Israel*, and particularly *the salvation of Israel*. The first occurrence in the Hebrew Bible of the idea of God as the Father comes when Moses marches in boldly to stand before Pharaoh, and says: Thus says YHWH: Israel is my son, my firstborn; let my people go, that they may serve me (Exodus 4.22-3). For

Israel to call God 'Father', then, was to hold on to the hope of liberty. The slaves were called to be sons.

When Jesus tells his disciples to call God 'Father', then, those with ears to hear will understand. He wants us to get ready for the new Exodus. We are going to be free at last. This is the Advent hope, the hope of the coming of the Kingdom of God. The tyrant's grip is going to be broken, and we shall be free:

I see my light come shining,
From the west down to the east.
Any day now – any day now –
I shall be released.

The very first word of the Lord's Prayer, therefore (in Greek or Aramaic, 'Father' would come first), contains within it not just intimacy, but revolution. Not just familiarity; hope.

The other strong echo of 'Father' within Jesus' world reinforces and fills out this revolutionary, kingdom-bearing meaning. God promised to King David that from his family there would come a child who would rule over God's people and whose kingdom would never be shaken. Of this coming King, God said to David, 'I will his Father, and he shall be my Son' (2 Samuel 7.14). The Messiah, the King that would come, would focus in himself God's promise to the whole people. And in Isaiah this promise, though still affirmed, is thrown open to all God's people. 'If anyone is thirsty, let them come and drink. . . and I will make with them an everlasting covenant, my steadfast, sure love for David' (Isaiah 55.1, 3). The two pictures go together. Freedom for Israel in bondage will come about through the liberating work of the Messiah. And Jesus, picking up all these resonances, is saying to his followers: this is *your* prayer. You are the liberty-people. You are the Messianic people.

You see, the Jews had clung on to that Exodus-hope, down through the years in which they still lived with slavery, with exile, with the awful sense that the promises were taking a mighty long time to be fully fulfilled. 'Surely you are our Father', says one of the later prophecies, 'though Abraham does not know us, and Israel does not acknowledge us' (Isaiah 63.16). In other words, the national hope seems to have slipped away; the things we thought were so secure have turned to dust and ashes; yet we cling on to the fact that you are our Father, and that fact gives us hope where humanly there is no hope. Assyria, Babylon, Persia, Greece, Egypt, Syria, and now

Rome; when would the tyranny of evil end? When would Israel be free? Most Jews knew in their bones, because they celebrated it at Passover and sang about it in the Psalms, that freedom would come when God gave them the new, final Exodus. Many believed that this would happen when the Messiah came. The very first word of the Lord's Prayer says: Let it be *now*; and let it be *us*. Father. . . *Our Father*. . .

Jesus' own life and work and teaching, then, was not simply about a timeless new vision of God. Jesus didn't come simply to offer a new pattern, or even a new depth, of spirituality. Spiritual depth and renewal come, as and when they come, as part of the larger package. But that package itself is about being delivered from evil; about return from exile; about having enough bread; about God's kingdom coming on earth as it is in heaven. It's the Advent-package. Jesus was taking the enormous risk of saying that this package was coming about through his own work. All of that is contained in the word 'Father', used in this way, within this prayer.

For Jesus, it was a great wager of faith and vocation. It meant leaving the security of home, family and job because his Father was calling him to a new job. He called the fishermen to become fishers of men. He himself, the carpenter, was called to take wood and nails to accomplish the real Exodus, the real defeat of evil. Calling God 'Father' was not simply comfortable or reassuring. It contained the ultimate personal challenge.

That is why, in the Garden of Gethsemane, he called God 'Father' once more. In John's gospel Jesus uses the image of father and son to explain what he was himself doing. In that culture, the son is apprenticed to the father. He learns his trade by watching what the father is doing. When he runs into a problem, he checks back to see how his father tackles it. That's what Jesus is doing in Gethsemane, when everything suddenly goes dark on him. Father, is this the way? Is this really the right path? Do I really have to drink this cup? The letter to the Hebrews says, with considerable daring, that the Son 'learned obedience by what he suffered' (Hebrews 5.7–9; compare 2.10–18). What we see in Gethsemane is the apprentice son, checking back one more time to see how the Father is doing it. And what is the project that Father and Son together are engaged upon? Nothing less than the new Exodus, rescuing Israel and the whole world from evil, injustice, fear and sin. The daring thing about that passage in Hebrews is this: Jesus too, like us, *went on learning* what it actually meant to call God 'Father'. And the learning process was only complete when he said, 'Father, into your hands I commend my spirit.'

The word 'Father', then, concentrates our attention on the doubly revolutionary message and mission of Jesus. It is the Exodus-message, the message that tyrants and oppressors rightly fear. But it isn't a message of simple human revolution. Most revolutions breed new tyrannies; not this one. This is the Father's revolution. It comes through the suffering and death of the Son. That's why, at the end of the Lord's Prayer, we pray to be delivered from the great tribulation; which is, not surprisingly, what Jesus told his disciples to pray for in the garden. This revolution comes about through the Messiah, and his people, sharing and bearing the pain of the world, that the world may be healed. This is the kingdom-message, the Advent-message.

But if we in turn are to be the messengers, we need to learn to pray this prayer. We, too, need to learn what it means to call God 'Father', and we mustn't be surprised when we find ourselves startled by what it means. The one thing you can be sure of with God is that you can't predict what he's going to do next. That's why calling God 'Father' is the great act of faith, of holy boldness, of risk. Saying 'our father' isn't just the boldness, the sheer cheek, of walking into the presence of the living and almighty God and saying 'Hi, Dad.' It is the boldness, the sheer total risk, of saying quietly 'Please may I, too, be considered an apprentice son.' It means signing on for the Kingdom of God.

This is what Jesus meant when he gave us this prayer. At the end of John's gospel, Jesus says to his followers: As the Father sent me, so I send you (John 20.21). We live between Advent and Advent; between the first great Advent, the coming of the Son into the world, and the second Advent, when he shall come again in power and glory to judge the living and the dead. That's why Advent is sometimes quite confusing, preparing for the birth of Jesus and at the same time preparing for the time when God makes all things new, when the whole cosmos has its exodus from slavery. That apparent confusion, that overlap of the first and second Advents, is actually what Christianity is all about: celebrating the decisive victory of God, in Jesus Christ, over Pharaoh and the Red Sea, over sin and death –and looking for, and working for, and longing for, and praying for, the full implementation of that decisive victory. Every Eucharist catches exactly this tension. 'As often as you break the bread and drink the cup, you proclaim, you announce, the death of the Lord – until he comes' (1 Corinthians 11.26). We come for our daily, and heavenly, bread; we come for our daily, and final, forgiveness; we come for our daily, and ultimate, deliverance; we come to celebrate God's kingdom *now*, and to pray for it *soon*. That is what we mean when we call God 'Father'.

And as we do this, as we pray this prayer in this setting, we begin to discover the true pattern of Christian spirituality, of the Christian way of penetrating into the mystery, of daring to enter the cloud of unknowing. When we call God 'Father', we are called to step out, as apprentice children, into a world of pain and darkness. We will find that darkness all around us; it will terrify us, precisely because it will remind us of the darkness inside our own selves. The temptation then is to switch off the news, to shut out the pain of the world, to create a painless world for ourselves. A good deal of our contemporary culture is designed to do exactly that. No wonder people find it hard to pray. But if, as the people of the living creator God, we respond to the call to be his sons and daughters; if we take the risk of calling him Father; then we are called to be the people through whom the pain of the world is held in the healing light of the love of God. And we then discover that we want to pray, and need to pray, this prayer. Father; Our

Father; Our Father in heaven; Our Father in heaven, may your name be honoured. That is, may you be worshipped by your whole creation; may the whole cosmos resound with your praise; may the whole world be freed from injustice, disfigurement, sin, and death, and *may your name be hallowed*. And as we stand in the presence of the living God, with the darkness and pain of the world on our hearts, praying that he will fulfill his ancient promises, and implement the victory of Calvary and Easter for the whole cosmos – then we may discover that our own pain, our own darkness, is somehow being dealt with as well.

This, then, I dare say, is the pattern of Christian spirituality. It is not the selfish pursuit of private spiritual advancement. It is not the flight of the alone to the alone. It is neither simply shouting into a void, nor simply getting in touch with our own deepest feelings, though sometimes it may feel like one or other of these. It is the rhythm of standing in the presence of the pain of the world, and kneeling in the presence of the creator of the world; of bringing those two things together in the name of Jesus and by the victory of the cross; of living in the tension of the double Advent, and of calling God 'Father'.

Jesus took the risk of referring to God obliquely. In John's gospel, one of his regular ways of talking about God was 'the Father who sent me.' He wanted people to discover who the Father really was by seeing what he, Jesus, was doing. When we call God 'Father', we are making the same astonishing, crazy, utterly risky claim. The mission of the church is contained in that word; the failure of the church is highlighted by that word. But the failure, too, is taken care of in the prayer, and in the cross. Our task is to grow up into the Our Father, to dare to impersonate our older brother, seeking daily bread and daily forgiveness as we do so: to wear his clothes, to walk in his shoes, to feast at his table, to weep with him in the garden, to share his suffering, and to know his victory. As our Saviour Jesus Christ has commanded and taught us, by his life and death, even more than by his words, we are bold, very bold, – even crazy, some might think – to say 'Our Father'.

# CHAPTER TWO

# Thy Kingdom Come

What are we praying *for* when we pray for God's Kingdom to come?

The second main petition in the Lord's Prayer – 'Thy Kingdom Come' – rules out any idea that the Kingdom of God is a purely heavenly (that is, 'other-worldly') reality. Thy kingdom come, we pray, thy will be done, *on earth as it is in heaven*. Sort out the familiar, but technical, terms. 'Heaven' and 'earth' are the two interlocking arenas of God's good world. Heaven is God's space, where God's writ runs and God's future purposes are waiting in the wings. Earth is our world, our space. Think of the vision at the end of Revelation. It isn't about humans being snatched up from earth to heaven. The holy city, new Jerusalem, comes down *from* heaven to earth. God's space and ours are finally married, integrated at last.

That is what we pray for when we pray 'thy Kingdom come'.

Jesus' contemporaries were longing for God to become King. Putting it bluntly, they were fed up with the other kings they'd had for long enough. As far as they were concerned, the Roman emperors were a curse, and the Herodian dynasty was a joke. It was time for the true God, the true King, to step into history, to take the power and the glory, to claim the Kingdom for his own.

The prophets had promised it. Ezekiel: YHWH himself will come to be the shepherd of Israel. Zechariah: YHWH will come, and all his saints with him. Malachi (with more than a tinge of warning): the Lord, whom ye seek, will suddenly come to his Temple. And, towering over them all, Isaiah: there will be a highway in the wilderness; the valleys and mountains will be flattened out; the glory of YHWH shall be revealed, and all flesh shall see it together. Zion hears her watchmen shouting 'Here is your God!' Isaiah's message holds together the majesty and gentleness of this god who comes in power and who comes to feed his flock like a shepherd, carrying the lambs, and gently leading the mother sheep. This is the kingdom-message Jesus lived by; this prophetic vision is the basis of the Lord's Prayer.

But what will it mean, when Israel's God returns to be King? According to the same prophetic passages, there will be a new Exodus: the evil empire will be defeated, and God's people will be free.

> How lovely on the mountains are the feet of the messenger who brings good news, who announces salvation, who says to Zion 'Your God reigns.' Listen! Your watchmen lift up their voices, together they sing for joy; for in plain sight they see the return of YHWH to Zion. YHWH has bared his holy arm in the sight of all the nations; and all the ends of the earth shall see the salvation of our God. (Isaiah 52.7–10)

Jesus, I think, knew these prophecies intimately, and deliberately made them the theme of his own work. When we sing of Zion hearing the watchmen's voices, we are singing the song Jesus himself had in mind as he told his followers to pray, *Thy Kingdom Come.*

So was Jesus' kingdom-message, after all, simply about national and political liberation?

At this point Western Christianity has tended to say: of course not. Jesus wasn't into politics; he came with a spiritual message, the timeless and eternal truths of personal salvation. Well, that clearly won't do. We'd have to cut out the tell-tale phrase, *on earth, as it is in heaven*. Whatever Jesus' Kingdom-announcement was all about, it was about something that actually *happens*, within the space-time world. But, equally, Jesus' parables regularly challenged the simple one-dimensional liberationist kingdom-vision that his contemporaries cherished. If Isaiah's message is about God's healing for the nations, about Israel being the light of the world, this will not be achieved by military victory. To put it crudely, how can the Prince of Peace defeat evil if he has to abandon Peace itself in order to do so?

No. Jesus took the three parts of Isaiah's kingdom-message and set about implementing them. Release for captive Israel; the defeat of evil; and the return of YHWH to Zion.

First, release for captive Israel. Jesus tells a story of a son who goes off in disgrace into a pagan country, and who is welcomed back, astonishingly, with open arms and a huge party. For Jesus' first hearers, 'the Prodigal Son' wasn't just a timeless message of repentance and forgiveness. It was, rather, the story of the new Exodus, the liberation of captive Israel. But Jesus, in telling this story, was not issuing a call to arms in the struggle for liberty. He was explaining why he was constantly celebrating the Kingdom with the outcasts and misfits. Somehow, he seemed to be saying, through his strange work the kingdom was appearing, even though it didn't look like people had imagined. This was how the captives were being released.

Second, Jesus spoke and acted as if evil's long reign would finally be defeated through his own work. (We shall look at this in Chapter 4.) Isaiah's Kingdom-message promised defeat for the evil regime which had enslaved God's people. Woven into that message, in Isaiah, we find four poems about a strange character, the Servant of the Lord, who will be God's agent in accomplishing this task. The prophecy as a whole (Isaiah 40—55) sets out the promise of the Kingship of God; the Servant-songs, within it, set out a job description for how the promise is to be realised. Jesus volunteered for the job. This, he believed, was how evil would be defeated.

Thirdly, Isaiah had declared that YHWH himself would return to his people: coming with power and justice, coming gentle as a shepherd. Jesus spoke of his own work in the same terms. He frequently explained what he was doing in terms of a shepherd rescuing lost sheep. He told stories about a king, or a master, returning to his servants to see what they were up to. Jesus spoke and acted as if he was called to embody not just the return from exile, not just the defeat of evil, but also, astonishingly, the return of YHWH to Zion.

Jesus, then, embraced a crazy and utterly risky vocation. And when he taught his disciples to pray, Thy Kingdom Come, he wanted them to pray that he would succeed in it.

That prayer, astonishingly, was answered. They thought it hadn't been; but Easter proved them wrong. Jesus' first followers, to their own great surprise, quickly came to believe that God's kingdom *had* come, and his will *had* been done – in Palestine, in Jerusalem, on Calvary, and in the Easter Garden. Heaven and earth had finally dovetailed together. The prophecies had been fulfilled, though not at all in the way they had expected.

Jesus' first followers didn't think, for a moment, that the Kingdom meant simply some new religious advice – an improved spirituality, a better code of morals, or a freshly crafted theology. They held to a stronger, and more dangerous, claim. They believed that in the unique life, death and resurrection of Jesus the whole cosmos had turned the corner from darkness to light. The Kingdom was indeed here, though it differed radically from what they had imagined.

And of course they faced the question: if the Kingdom is here, why is there still injustice? Why is there
still hunger? Why is there still guilt? Why is there
still evil? They didn't dodge this question. They
didn't escape into saying: oh, we didn't mean that;
we're talking about a new individual spiritual experience, leading to us sharing God's kingdom in heaven,
not on earth. No. They went on praying *and living*
the Lord's Prayer. And they would tell us to do the
same.

But how? What Jesus did, he did uniquely, once
and for all. That is essential to the gospel. We don't
have to go on repeating it again and again; and we
couldn't, even if we wanted to. Rather, think of it
like this. Jesus is the medical genius who discovered
penicillin; we are doctors, ourselves being cured by
the medicine, now applying it to those who need it.
Jesus is the musical genius who wrote the greatest
oratorio of all time; we are the musicians, captivated
by his composition ourselves, who now perform it
before a world full of muzak and cacophany. The
Kingdom did indeed come with Jesus; but it will fully
come when the world is healed, when the whole creation finally joins in the song. But it must be Jesus'
medicine; it must be Jesus' music. And the only way
to be sure of that is to pray his prayer.

What then might it mean to pray this Kingdom-prayer today?

It means, for a start, that as we look up into the face of our Father in Heaven, and commit ourselves to the hallowing of his name, that we look immediately out upon the whole world that he made, and we see it as he sees it. Thy Kingdom Come: to pray this means seeing the world in binocular vision. See it with the love of the creator for his spectacularly beautiful creation; and see it with the deep grief of the creator for the battered and battle-scarred state in which the world now finds itself. Put those two together, and bring the binocular picture into focus: the love and the grief join into the Jesus-shape, the kingdom-shape, the shape of the cross – never was Love, dear King, never was Grief like thine! And, with this Jesus before your eyes, pray again, *Thy Kingdom Come, thy will be done, on earth as it is in heaven!* We are praying, as Jesus was praying and acting, for the redemption of the world; for the radical defeat and uprooting of evil; and for heaven and earth to be married at last, for God to be all in all. And if we pray this way, we must of course be prepared to live this way.

So, as we pray this for the world, we also pray it, of course, for the church. But this cannot simply mean that we want God to sort out our messes and muddles, so that the church can be a cosy place, without problems or pain. We can only pray this prayer for the church if we are prepared to mean: make us Kingdom-bearers! Make us a community of healed healers; make us a retuned orchestra to play the Kingdom-music until the world takes up the song. Make us, in turn, Servants of the Lord, the few with the message for the many.

The world, the church – but what of ourselves?

I used to think of this clause simply as a prayer of resignation. 'Thy will be done', with a shrug of the shoulders: what I want doesn't matter too much; if God really wants to do something I suppose I can put up with it. That might do if God were a remote, detached, God. It won't do for Isaiah's God; it won't do for Jesus; and it won't do for those who break bread and drink wine to remember Jesus and pray for the kingdom. No: this is the risky, crazy prayer of submission and commission, or, if you like, the prayer of subversion and conversion. It is the way we sign on, in our turn, for the work of the kingdom. It is the way we take the medicine ourselves, so that we may be strong enough to administer it to others. It is the way we retune our instruments, to play God's oratorio for the world to sing.

There is one important spin-off of this. Along with the unbiblical view of the Kingdom that sees it as the escape from the created order, rather than the redemption of it, there is a view of prayer that sees it as essentially the activity of the mind, the heart, or the soul, leaving the body untouched and irrelevant. This view has a certain strength: it will never fall into ritualism or magic, or into thinking that we can put on a pretty little outward show which God will then politely applaud.

But that's actually about all that can be said for it. Thy Kingdom Come *on earth* as it is in heaven; and we who pray that prayer are ourselves bits of earth, lumps of clay. If we really want God's kingdom to come on earth, we should of course expect that the earth in question will include *this* earth, this clay, this present physical body. That means, of course, holiness. It means, of course, sacraments. And, held between holiness and sacraments, it means the *physical* act of prayer.

Sadly for those who like everything tidy, there are no rules at this point. Some, after all, find kneeling difficult; some can't stand for very long; some are too shy to cross themselves or raise their hands into the Orthodox praying position or its recent Charismatic cousin; some realise that their flamboyance in doing these things may be a hindrance to anxious neighbours; and so on. But this doesn't mean that the physical expression of prayer is irrelevant. We have learnt a lot in our generation about what we call 'body language'; have we thought of applying it to our prayer?

If we do, we may well discover that the great men and women of prayer in other times and cultures had learnt a trick or two. The ideal posture, they would tell us, is relaxed but not slumped; poised but not tense; alert but not fidgety; above all, humble but happy in the presence of the Creator whom you are learning to call 'Father'. Find the posture that does all that for you; find the gestures that express and symbolize the life and love of Jesus for you; and you will be teaching your body to pray – which, to the surprise of many modern persons, is no bad way to teach your mind, heart and soul to pray as well. What is more, you will be acting out, in one little but vital local instance, the prayer you want to pray anyway: Thy Kingdom Come, *on earth as it is in heaven*. If we each learnt a bit more about how to do that, the medicine and the music of the gospel might make fresh inroads into the sick and cacophanous world all around us. And an excellent way to start is the acted drama of the liturgy; particularly, of course, our coming with empty and outstretched hands to take and taste the life and death and rising of Jesus.

You see, if it was part of Jesus' task to teach his followers to pray in this way, it is in a sense *our* task to teach the *world* to pray in this way. How might we get the opportunity? In Luke's gospel, Jesus waited until his followers asked him for a prayer; and the reason they asked was because *they saw what he was doing*. Something tells me there's a lesson there.

# CHAPTER THREE

# Give Us This Day

The danger with the prayer for bread is that we get there too soon.

We come to prayer, aware of urgent needs, or at least wants. It's tempting to race through the Lord's Prayer, as far as 'on earth as it is in heaven', so that we can then take a deep breath and say 'Now look here: when it comes to daily bread, there are some things I simply must have.' And then off we go into a shopping list. To do this, of course, is to let greed get in the way of grace.

When that happens, greed defeats its own object. If we don't spend time adoring our Father in heaven, seeking the honour of his name, and praying for his kingdom, all our own desires and hopes will simply present themselves to us in a muddled and jumbled fashion, coming bubbling up to the surface in what

C. S. Lewis, contemptuous of the later writings of James Joyce, called '*steam* of consciousness'.

Now don't misunderstand me. There is something perfectly valid in what you might call 'steaming in the presence of God'. If you feel as though you're boiling over, at least have the grace to come and do it in the presence of your Father in heaven. But, as the regular practice for our cooler moments, I suggest that we owe it to ourselves, not to mention to God, to pray the prayer in a more integrated manner.

We find the true depth of this petition by going back once more to the life of Jesus himself.

They said a lot of things about Jesus during his lifetime, by no means all complimentary. One particularly juicy phrase sticks out: he was, they said, 'a glutton and a winebibber'. You can just see Jesus' opponents rolling that one round their tongues with relish. But do you know where the phrase comes from? It's actually a quotation from Deuteronomy 21, in which the Israelites are told what to do with a stubborn and rebellious son. The parents are to bring him to the elders of the town, and say 'This son of ours is stubborn and rebellious. He will not obey us. He is a glutton and a winebibber', and they must stone him to death. So there was more to the charge against Jesus than just that he went to too many parties. It was a way of saying: he is being profoundly disloyal to our traditions; he deserves to die.

But Jesus was following the agenda he set out in the Lord's Prayer. He wasn't a rebellious son; he was loyal to the one *he* called 'Father'. His eating and drinking with his motley collection of friends was a deliberate sign of the Kingdom. His parties weren't simply a matter of cracking open another bottle for the sake of it; and the prayer to the Father for daily bread was part of his wider and deeper agenda.

At the heart of it stood a central biblical symbol of the kingdom: the great festive banquet which God has prepared for his people. This picture goes back to the vision of the land flowing with milk and honey; to the Psalmist, saying 'Thou shalt prepare a table before me, in the presence of my foes'; to the children of Israel, being fed with quails and manna in the wilderness; to prophecies like that of Isaiah, that

> On this mountain the LORD of hosts will make for
> all peoples
> a feast of rich food, a feast of well-aged wines.
> And he will destroy on this mountain
> the shroud over all people;
> he will swallow up death for ever.
> He will wipe away the tears from all faces,

and the disgrace of his people
he will take away from all the earth.
(Isaiah 25.6–8)

The banquet, the party, is a sign that God is acting at last, to rescue his people and wipe away all tears from all eyes. Jesus' parties, and his feeding of his followers in the wilderness, were intended, for those with eyes to see, to pick up this whole theme and celebrate it. As so often, the most powerful things Jesus said were in actions, not words.

Why then did they criticize him? Because, first, he was celebrating the feast of the kingdom *with all the wrong people*. He threw great parties for the most notorious of sinners. He went to eat with Zacchaeus, while the respectable burghers of Jericho tut-tutted on the pavement outside. And, in one famous passage, he explained these odd celebrations by telling stories – about lost sheep being found, lost coins being discovered, and about two lost sons being confronted by a Father's love. The angels, he said, were having a party over what was going on, so it was only right that he should, too (Luke 15.1–2, 7, 10, 23–4, 32). Jesus was re-inventing the Kingdom of God around his own work; and at the heart of it was the great sign of welcome to all-comers, welcome to the party, to the Messianic Banquet, to the renewed people of God. Jesus was offering all and sundry the daily bread that spoke of the Kingdom of God.

But if Jesus was celebrating with all the wrong people, he was also, from his contemporaries' point of view, celebrating *at exactly the wrong time*. The Jews of Jesus' day kept various fast days, commemorating moments of great sadness in Israel's history. But Jesus refused to fast on those days. Instead, he threw parties. By way of explanation, he spoke of the wedding-guests being unable to fast as long as they had the Bridegroom with them. He was celebrating the great wedding-banquet of the Kingdom of God. You can't look miserable and keep fasting while that's going on. Jesus was celebrating the strange presence of God's Kingdom. And the prayer he gave his followers was a prayer for the complete fulfilment of that Kingdom: for God's people to be rescued from hunger, guilt and fear. 'Give us this day our daily bread' means, in this setting, 'Let the party continue.'

This should help us to understand the interesting difference, in this clause of the prayer, between Matthew's and Luke's versions. The Greek is tricky, but Matthew's seems to mean 'give us *today* our bread for *tomorrow*'; while Luke understands it as 'give us *each day* our daily bread'. They both probably reflect different aspects of what Jesus intended. Matthew, in line with Jesus' whole agenda, means 'give us, *here and now*, the bread of life which is promised for the great Tomorrow'. Give us, in other words, the blessings of the coming Kingdom – right now. Matthew, writing his gospel, saw this prayer partially answered in the feedings of the five thousand and the four thousand; more fully in the Last Supper; and, most fully of all, in Jesus' death and resurrection.

But Luke's version is not to be sneezed at as merely one-dimensional, just praying for boring old bread. The whole point of the Kingdom, as we saw in the previous chapter, is that it isn't about shifting our wants and desires on to a non-physical level, moving away from the earthly to the supposedly 'spiritual'. It is about God's dimension coming to birth within ours, which is after all what Advent and Christmas are anticipating and celebrating. The Kingdom is to come *in earth as it is in heaven*. Daily needs and desires point beyond themselves, to God's promise of the kingdom in which death and sorrow will be no more. But that means, too, that the promise of the Kingdom *includes* those needs, and doesn't look down on them sneeringly as somehow second-rate.

This clause of the prayer thus becomes a window on four central issues in our own praying.

Consider, first, what to do with the muddled jumble, the steam of consciousness, that I spoke of earlier. Clear your mind to pray, and what do you find? A buzz of fears and hopes and wants and puzzles; behind that, perhaps, some deep sadnesses; some real anger – and, I hope, some real joy, some true delight. What are we to do with all these devices and desires?

One of the most telling prayers in Cranmer's liturgy comes at the start of his great Communion service: Almighty God, to whom all hearts are open, all desires known, and from whom no secrets are hid. . . *All desires known*. How do you react to that? You can tell a great deal about your spiritual health by enquiring whether you see those words as a promise, or as a threat.

Those who feel deeply threatened by God knowing all our desires will naturally want the Lord's Prayer to be about 'spiritual' issues. If I'm ashamed of my desires, and would prefer God *not* to know them, then it will be much more comfortable for me if the 'daily bread' for which I pray is for the soul, rather than the stomach. But Jesus doesn't leave us that option. Jesus does, of course, warn his hearers not to spend all their energy working simply for the food which perishes, but to strive instead for the food which lasts to eternal life. But he doesn't make this point by denying them food for the stomach; he provides for them at that level, and points, through that, to a deeper provision for deeper needs and desires. In his knowledge of their needs, for bread and all else besides, is no threat, but only promise.

Scripture, says Paul, is given so that by its encouragement we might have hope. Scripture is full of stories of people who brought their deep natural longings into the presence of God, and found them answered by being taken up within his purposes. Naomi longed that her daughter-in-law Ruth might have a husband; God, answering that longing, made Ruth the great-grandmother of King David, the man after his own heart. Hannah longed for a child; God gave her Samuel, who would become his mouthpiece to Israel. The disciples, in Acts 1, were longing for Israel to become the world's great nation; Jesus answered that culture-bound, political hope in a totally unexpected way, sending them out as his royal ambassadors to announce him as the new worldwide King.

'Give us this day our daily bread'; this clause in the Lord's Prayer, then, reminds us that our natural longings, for bread and all that it symbolizes, are not to be shunned as though they were of themselves evil. Of course a genuine glutton must repent of desiring, and grabbing, more bread than is wise or good. But

God knows our desires in order that we may turn them into prayer; in order that they may be sorted out, straightened out, untangled and reaffirmed. If we truly pray this prayer, with due weight to each clause, we are taking the first steps from the chaos of our normal interior life towards an order and clarity which will let the joy come through to the surface.

The Kingdom-prayer isn't a prayer, such as some religions would advocate, for our desires to be taken away or annihilated. In bringing them into the prayer within the setting of the earlier petitions for God's honour, his kingdom and his will, it asks for our desires to be satisfied in God's way and God's time. And, since God himself is most truly the deepest object of our hunger, this clause asks that we may be fed with God himself. And there can be no question of God failing to answer this prayer. 'Breathe through the heats of our desires thy coolness and thy balm.'

Second, this clause reminds us that God intends us to pray for specific needs. It is, no doubt, much easier to pray 'God bless everyone' than to pray 'Please bring peace to the Middle East'. It may seem more 'spiritual' to pray for the conversion of the world than for a parking space near to the meeting for which we're about to be late. Now of course we would trivialize Christian prayer if we thought it was *only* about praying for parking spaces, for our team to win the match, or for fine weather for the church fête. But, once we put the prayer for daily bread within the whole kingdom-prayer where it belongs, to turn then to the specific things we honestly need right now is not trivial. It is precisely what children do when they love and trust the one they call 'Father'.

Third, however, we must of course lift our eyes beyond our own needs. It is impossible truly to pray for our daily bread, or for tomorrow's bread today, without being horribly aware of the millions who didn't have bread yesterday, don't have any today, and in human terms are unlikely to have any tomorrow either. But what can we do about this, as we pray this prayer in church and go home to our Sunday lunch?

Well, obviously, we can give, as best we can. Obviously, we can become more politically sensitive and active, to support programmes not just for foreign aid but for a juster and fairer global economy. This is part of what it means to pray this prayer. But, in addition, we should be praying this prayer not just *for* the hungry, but *with* the hungry, and all who are desperate from whatever deep need. We should see ourselves, as we pray the Lord's Prayer, as part of the wider Christian family, and human family, standing alongside the hungry, and praying, in that sense, on their behalf.

We offer ourselves, in this prayer, as representatives of this world (this is what it means to be 'a royal priesthood'), turning into words the unspoken prayer from thousands of hungry folk in our own country and millions around the world, turning it into words that plead with our heavenly Father to feed the hungry, to care for the desperate. And when we have prayed in that fashion, the test of whether we were sincere will of course be whether we are prepared to stand physically alongside those for whom we have claimed to speak. This is, after all, a dangerous and subversive prayer to pray; but it's the one Jesus taught us. And, this time, the danger with the prayer for bread is that we get there too late.

Fourthly, all these aspects of prayer come together most obviously when we meet around the Lord's Table, when by the power of the Spirit bread and wine become the vehicles and vessels of God's own love in Jesus Christ. The Eucharist is, in a sense, both the highest form *of* prayer, and the first and most basic answer *to* our prayer. It forms a lens through which all the other answers come into focus.

The Eucharist is, first, the way in which Jesus himself taught us to remember him, to think of him.

If the Lord's Prayer is the *prayer* which summed up his own life and work, enabling his followers to breathe in his life and love and make it their own, the Eucharist is the *symbol* which did the same thing, pointing particularly to his dying and rising. As we do this in remembrance of him, we are taken back in heart and mind, and in sacramental time and place, to the very life of Jesus himself, as he feasted with his friends, as he celebrated one last kingdom-party. This is the Kingdom-banquet, and we are the honoured guests. That, as we saw, is where this clause in the prayer began.

But the Eucharist is also the place above all where we can come with our own physical, psychological, emotional and spiritual needs, and lay them before the God to whom all desires are known. The drama of what we do here, coming with empty hands to receive bread – God's bread, the bread of life, the bread of tomorrow which is Jesus Christ himself – this drama draws together in a deep and rich symbol the whole action by which we bring our muddled and jumbled selves into the light and love of God. We can bring whatever is on our minds and hearts to God in this action, without fear or shame, be our concerns never so agonizing or never so trivial, trusting that, along with the physical bread, the God we call 'Father' will

give us all that we need, not least healing, forgiveness, support, and courage, in every other depart-
ment of our lives.

So, finally, the Eucharist is the place where,
precisely as the people of Christ, we have the
responsibility to come on behalf of those in desperate
need, not least hunger. Jesus celebrated the Kingdom
by sharing his feasts with all sorts of people. So
should we. Here is a practical suggestion; it's only a
start, but it's better to start somewhere than to leave
everything at the level of grand general ideas. The
next time you come to the Eucharist, bring with you,
in mind and heart, someone you know, or know of,
or have seen on television, who desperately needs
God's bread, literally or metaphorically, today. Bring
them with you; let them kneel, in your mind's eye,
with you at the altar rail; and let them share the bread
and wine with you. And, as you return, strengthened
by God's food, ask yourself what this new friend
would mean when she or he prays 'Give me this day
my daily bread'. Then ask how you might be part of
God's answer to that prayer.

After all, we ourselves are only at Jesus' table
because he made a habit of celebrating parties with all
the wrong people. Isn't it about time we started to
copy him?

# CHAPTER FOUR

# Forgive Us Our Trespasses

One of the most vivid images in the whole New Testament is that of a man running.

These days, people of all sorts run to keep fit. Even presidents and politicians have been known to don jogging suits, and even to be photographed taking exercise. But in Jesus' world, the more senior you were in a community, the less likely you were even to walk fast. It shows a lack of dignity, of *gravitas*.

So when Jesus told a story about a man running, this was designed to have the same effect on his audience as we would experience if, say, the Prime Minister were to show up for the state opening of Parliament wearing a bathing costume. It's a total loss of dignity.

And when we discover why this man is running, the effect is even more shocking. This man is running to greet someone: someone who has put a curse on him, who has brought disgrace on the whole family. We call it the Parable of the Prodigal Son (Luke 15.11–32), but it might equally be called the Parable of the Running Father.

And only when we understand why this man is running will we really understand what Jesus meant when he taught us to pray: Forgive us our trespasses, as we forgive those who trespass against us.

We need shocking stories like the Running Father, because our generation has either forgotten about forgiveness or trivialized it. Once you replace morality with the philosophy that says 'if it feels good, do it', there isn't anything to forgive; if you still feel hurt by something, our culture suggests that you should simply retreat into your private world and pretend it didn't happen. In that sort of world, I don't need God to forgive me, and I don't need to forgive anybody else, either. Or, if people do still think about forgiveness, they seldom get beyond the small-scale private forgiveness of small-scale private sins. They hope God will forgive their peccadillos, and they try at least to smile benignly on their neighbours' follies.

Instead of genuine forgiveness, our generation has been taught the vague notion of 'tolerance'. This is, at best, a low-grade parody of forgiveness. At worst, it's a way of sweeping the real issues in human life under the carpet. If the Father in the story had intended merely to *tolerate* the son, he would not have been running down the road to meet him. Forgiveness is richer and higher and harder and more shocking than we usually think. Jesus' message offers the genuine article, and insists that we should accept no man-made substitutes.

So what was Jesus getting at, not only with that story but with the work he was doing, which the story was explaining? And how can we turn that story, and the reality to which it points, into prayer, as we pray the prayer Jesus taught us?

We have already seen that Jesus was announcing God's Kingdom, God's Rule. God was at last liberating Israel from her slavery and thus setting the whole world back to rights. What his contemporaries wanted, politically, socially, culturally and economically, was the end of oppression and exile. But they never thought that those were the deepest things at stake. Oppression and exile, according to all the prophets, had come about because of Israel's sin. So, if Israel was set free from oppression and exile, that event of liberation would be, quite simply, *the forgiveness of sins*. People in prison will, no doubt, want forgiveness at all sorts of levels; but if the

Home Secretary were to run down the road to open
the prison gate and let them out (now there's a shocking idea), they would know in no uncertain terms that
they had been thoroughly pardoned, forgiven.

This comes out clearly in the gospel accounts of
John the Baptist. He was offering 'a baptism of
repentance for the forgiveness of sins.' This wasn't
just to enable individuals suffering from bad consciences to seek relief. To go through the Jordan was
to re-enact the Exodus. John's action suggests that
this was how Israel's God was redeeming his people.
John was heralding the real return from exile, 'the
Forgiveness of Sins' in that sense. He was getting the
people ready for the arrival of her God. And Jesus
told a story in which that arrival looked like a man
running down the road to greet his disgraced son.

Jesus took his point of origin from John, but he
made two radical departures. First, he took the message away from the Jordan and out into the streets
and villages. Second, he told people, in word and in
acted symbol, that what John had spoken of as coming shortly had now arrived. 'My child,' he says,
'your sins are forgiven'; the shock of that astonishing
announcement, made in a private house by someone
with no rabbinic training or priestly qualification, was
partly that Jesus was presuming to offer something

that was normally dispensed through the Temple, but also because he was saying that 'the Forgiveness of Sins', the great act of liberation, had actually arrived.

Who does he think he is? they quite naturally asked. The obvious answer is: Jesus thinks he's the Kingdom-bringer. Jesus isn't just a 'teacher'; he is making an *announcement* about something that is *happening*; and he is doing and saying things which explain that announcement and demonstrate that it's true. 'My child, your sins are forgiven'; and he heals the man's paralysis. Jesus sits down to eat with tax-collectors and sinners, acting out the open welcome that Israel's God extends; when he's challenged about this undignified behaviour, he tells a story about a father who threw his dignity into the dustbin and ran down the road to welcome his disgraced son. Healings, parties, stories and symbols all said: the forgiveness of sins is happening, right under your noses. This is the new Exodus, the real Return from Exile, the prophetic fulfilment, the great liberation. This is the disgraceful Advent of our astonishing God.

So Jesus went from village to village, throughout the lovely Galilean countryside, announcing that the kingdom had arrived, that forgiveness of sins was happening, that God was transforming his people at last into the salt of the earth and the light of the world. And, wherever people responded to his call, he gave them instructions as to how they should live, as the new-Exodus people, the forgiveness-of-sins people. They were to live, in each village or town, as a cell of kingdom-people, a little group loyal to Jesus and his kingdom-vision.

In particular, having received God's forgiveness themselves, they were to practice it amongst themselves. Not to do so would mean they hadn't grasped what was going on. As soon as someone in one of these Jesus-cells refused to forgive a fellow-member, he or she was saying, in effect, 'I don't really believe the Kingdom has arrived. I don't think the Forgiveness of Sins has actually occurred.' Failure to forgive one another wasn't a matter of failing to live up to a new bit of moral teaching. It was cutting off the branch you were sitting on. The only reason for being Kingdom-people, for being Jesus' people, was that the forgiveness of sins was happening; so if you didn't live forgiveness, you were denying the very basis of your own new existence.

So the Lord's Prayer contains, at this point, a most unusual thing: a clause which commits the pray-er to actions which back up the petition just offered. 'Forgive us our trespasses, *as we forgive those who trespass against us*.' Prayer and life are here locked indissolubly together. And, please note: this *isn't* saying that we do this in order to *earn* God's forgiveness. It's a further statement of our loyalty to Jesus and his Kingdom. Claiming this central blessing of the Kingdom only makes sense if we are living by that same central blessing ourselves.

Among the many meanings which this had for Jesus' followers was that they were to practice the great old biblical command of Jubilee. Not only were they to forgive one another their sins and offences; they would have no debts from each other. This, indeed, is the clear meaning of the relevant word in Matthew's version of the Lord's Prayer: Forgive us our *debts*, as we forgive our debtors. You may perhaps say that, since the debt we owe to God is moral, not financial, Jesus must have been using this word as a metaphor. That is sometimes the case; but we can't escape the question so easily.

The problem of debt was very serious in Jesus' time. When the revolutionaries took over the Temple at the start of the Jewish war against the Romans, thirty years after Jesus' day, the first thing they did was to burn the records of debt. The early church certainly believed that Jesus was talking about actual debts. The Lord's Prayer makes sense, not just in terms of individual human beings quieting their own troubled consciences, vital though that is, but also in terms of the new day when justice and peace will embrace, economically and socially as well as personally and existentially.

So this clause in the prayer is anchored, like all the others, in the career and announcement of Jesus. As I've said before, the prayer is given so that Jesus' followers can breathe in what he's doing and so, with that breath, come alive with his life. How might this work with this clause in particular?

To begin with, we note that, from the point of view of Jesus' earliest followers, this prayer was supremely answered when Jesus was crucified. In the light of the resurrection, they came to see that the cross was indeed the great act of liberation, of forgiveness, for which they had been waiting, even though it certainly didn't look like it at the time. And we, as their heirs and successors, look back to that great event with gratitude, and celebrate it year by year and week by week as the true Exodus, the moment when the pain and the sin of all the world were heaped up into one place and dealt with for ever.

But if sins were forgiven once and for all when Jesus died on the cross, why is there still sin and evil in the world at all? And why should we go on praying this prayer day after day if we say, in creed and hymn, in liturgy and scripture, that it has already been answered?

The response to this question is that we are now called to be the people through whom the unique victory of Calvary and Easter is implemented in and for the whole world. The church is to be the advance guard of the great act of Forgiveness of Sins that God intends to accomplish for the entire cosmos. Justice and peace, truth and mercy, will one day reign in God's world; and the church, who could almost be defined as the people who pray the Lord's Prayer, is to model and pioneer the way of life which is, actually, the *only* way of life, because it is the way of forgiveness.

To pray this prayer is therefore, in its largest meaning, to pray for the world. 'Forgive us our trespasses': lift up your eyes for a moment, away from your own sins and those of your immediate neighbour, and see the world as a whole, groaning in travail, longing for peace and justice; see the endless tangles in which politicians and power-brokers get themselves, and the endless human misery which results; put yourself in the shoes of the peasant who has lost husband and home and faces a winter in the snow, or of the politician who discovers that he's in too deep and that all the options open are evil ones; of the men of violence who have forgotten that there was a different way to live. Collect all these images and roll them into one, that of a young Jewish boy off in the far country feeding the pigs; and then, with your courage in both hands, say 'Forgive us our trespasses': 'I will arise and go to my father, and will say to him, Father, I have sinned. . .' But, as you say it in your prayer, with the whole world of pain in view, allow your praying heart to see the next scene, with the Father doing the unthinkable, the disgraceful thing, and running down the road to meet his muddled and muddy son.

As we pray this prayer for the world, let us be alert to new visions of what the living God wants us to aim at in our society. Could it be that we could work and pray for a Jubilee, for the cancellation of the debts which are crippling half the world and keeping the other half in clover?

How might the second clause – 'as we forgive those who trespass against us' – work out in this context? We, as the people who pray this prayer for the world, are called to be the people who live in this way ourselves. At the end of Luke's gospel, Jesus sends the disciples to announce 'the forgiveness of sins' to the whole cosmos. The church is to tell, and to live, the Jubilee-message, the forgiveness-of-sins message. The church is to embody before the world the disgraceful, glorious, shocking and joyful message of the arrival of the King. When the world sees what the church is doing, it ought to ask questions to which the proper answer would be a story about a father running down the road to embrace his disreputable son. The second clause in the prayer is, therefore, a prayer of commitment to live in love and peace with all our Christian sisters and brothers. It is the prayer that should both undergird the ecumenical movement and remind us daily of the need to be reconciled within our own communities.

Well, you may say, the church seems to have drifted quite a long way from the mark. Yes, I guess we have; but it is never too late to lift up our eyes and recapture the vision, the vision of the God who comes. John the Baptist was the voice crying in the wilderness, preparing the way of the Lord, making straight in the desert a highway for God. The glory of the Lord shall be revealed, and all flesh shall see it together; yes, says Jesus, and this – the picture of the father running down the road – is what it will look like. And if the picture is darkened by the presence of the older brother, who very naturally stays sulking in a corner, muttering that there's no such thing as a free fatted calf, that shows that Jesus himself was well aware of the problems that stand between vision and reality, and of the need not just to welcome the disgraced son but to reassure the wounded and puzzled brother. That, too, is part of the prayer: if we pray from the point of view of the prodigal, we must learn to pray for all the older brothers, in church and world, who find at the moment that they simply can't join in the party.

How might this prayer affect us in our personal lives?

The first thing to say concerns the liturgy. Thomas Cranmer was so concerned to stress that we come to God as penitent sinners that, in his order for Mattins and Evensong, the first thing we do is to confess our sins. If you allow this to dictate your pattern of spirituality, there is a danger that you will think of yourself *permanently* as a prodigal son crawling home to be greeted by a rather stern father, who may perhaps be persuaded to let bygones be bygones. And that, of course, is a complete travesty of the whole parable.

And this problem provokes a reaction: 'Oh, that's all too gloomy! We don't need to bother about all that sin business; it's so morbid and unnecessary.' The balance of the Lord's Prayer corrects both these

extremes – as indeed Cranmer's own Communion
Service does. In both, we come into our Father's
presence as beloved children, ready to feast at his
table. Before the meal itself, of course, it is right that
we wash our hands: we still need to confess, and
receive absolution, within the larger framework of the
Father's glad welcome and the prospect of the banquet. Having been met with our Father's heartfelt
greeting, having expressed our love for him, and our
trust in him, we say, 'Now: there are one or two difficult things we need to sort out'. And God replies,
gently, 'Yes, there are, aren't there? Let's get them
out on the table and we'll deal with them.'

Notice what this balance achieves. How easy it is
for us to do one of three things with guilt, all of
which are ultimately no good. We can imagine guilt,
we can deny guilt, or we can simply live with guilt.
Each of these can cause a variety of spiritual and
psychological problems, not least depression and
anger (which can of course be caused by other things
as well). The Lord's Prayer clears away the paranoia
and gets us down to business. The sequence of
thought in the Prayer is designed to clear our eyes to
see which bits of our guilt are purely imaginary, and
which bits are real – and how we are to deal with the
latter. Once we face up to real guilt, we can deal with

it: by confessing it frankly and honestly, and by waking up again to the forgiving love of God as we see it in the life and death of Jesus. It's no good going to the doctor with imaginary ailments. But if there really is something wrong, it's better to let him deal with it.

In particular, it is better to let the doctor – and that's another image that Jesus used – deal with the hurts that others have inflicted on us. Everybody carries bruises, whether physical or emotional, from things that others have done. Often it was quite accidental; they didn't mean to hurt us; but what they did or said still rankles, still smoulders away in our memory. The only thing to do is to be frank about it before God. He, after all, had and has plenty of experience of people saying and doing things that hurt him. And with his healing for the hurt, and his help with the often long-drawn-out task of forgiveness, the bruises can be healed.

Of course, none of this is easy. If you've never set about it seriously, it may take time, and you may need help. That, after all, is one of the things that clergy are supposed to be there for – though a wise and prayerful lay friend may do the job just as well. There are books that may help. But the best help of all is the honest, careful praying of the Lord's Prayer.

It is our birthright, as the followers of Jesus, to breathe in true divine forgiveness day by day, as the cool, clear air which our spiritual lungs need instead of the grimy, germ-laden air that is pumped at us from all sides. And, once we start inhaling God's fresh air, there is a good chance that we will start to breathe it out, too. As we learn what it is like to be forgiven, we begin to discover that it is possible, and indeed joyful, to forgive others.

This breathing in of God's clean air is, of course, what we do in particular when we come to feast at Jesus' table. The Eucharist is the direct historical descendant, not just of the Last Supper, but of those happy and shocking parties which Jesus shared with all and sundry as a sign that they were surprisingly and dramatically forgiven. This meal, in other words, is linked directly to the meals which Jesus explained by telling the story of the Running Father. Hold that image in your mind as you come to Communion. Whichever far country you may be in, and for whatever reason, you don't have to stay there one moment longer. By the time you get to the words 'forgive us our trespasses', you will already have been embraced by the Father who has run down the road to meet you.

# CHAPTER FIVE

# Deliver Us From Evil

The previous chapter focussed on the Running Father, as we looked at the prayer for forgiveness. This time, as we come to the prayer for Deliverance from Evil, the dominant image offered to us is that of the Waiting Mother.

'The hopes and fears of all the years are met in thee tonight.' The Christmas hymn 'O Little Town of Bethlehem' uses these words of the city where Jesus was born; but we could use them just as well of Mary, the mother of Jesus. 'Behold, the handmaid of the Lord', she had said: and this is where it led. A dangerous journey at the wrong time of the year; the travel agent double-booking the hotel room; and then the hope and fear that had been trembling inside her for nine months focussing themselves on the great moment of pain and travail.

The pain of childbearing is at the heart of Mary's story: great hope, born through great fear. The imagery of Christmas Eve, such as hasn't been obliterated in our world by frantic preparations for the next day, properly includes the sense of the deep darkness before dawn, darkness before the Morning Star rises. For many Christians, for much of their life, this imagery sums up the way things are. The world is still out of joint; but we know that God's new world is to be born *through* present pain and travail. And we know this because we know the one who came into the world with a death sentence already hanging over him, as the paranoid old tyrant up the road got wind of a young royal pretender.

So it's scarcely surprising that, when the young pretender grew up, and proceeded to collect a rag-tag-and-bobtail royal retinue around him, he would give them, as their identifying badge, a prayer which included the urgent petition: Let us not be led into the Testing – but deliver us from Evil!

This prayer, like all the other petitions in the Lord's Prayer, is firmly grounded in the life and work of Jesus himself. Jesus, as we have seen, was deeply rooted in the hopes and fears of first-century Israel, clinging to the belief that she was the people of the true God. But what would this vocation mean?

Jewish visionaries, from the early prophets right up to Jesus' day and beyond, saw Israel's vocation in terms of a great build-up of pressure and pain. The night would get darker; then, when it was pitch black, when hope had died and fear had conquered, the morning star would dawn at last. The whole world, with Israel at its heart, would enter a period of tribulation, of sorrow and anguish, like that of a woman in labour; and from this the new world would be born, in which God's kingdom would come, and his will be done, on earth as it is in heaven. Israel's task was to say 'Behold, the handmaid of the Lord,' and so to become the vessel and vehicle of God's pain and travail, and of his triumph over evil.

Jesus took this theme, like so many others from his Jewish heritage, and drew its strings together into his own hand. Testing, temptation, and trial marked out his entire public life. He went straight off after his baptism, to wrestle with the huge and awesome implications of his newly-confirmed vocation. That wrestling focussed itself in a series of choices which, like all real rejections of real temptation, must have felt like cutting off a hand or plucking out an eye. He returned in the power of the Spirit, to announce the Kingdom. Wherever he went he was faced with opposition. Sometimes this took the form of tormented and benighted souls yelling and raving; sometimes it was equally tormented and benighted souls criticizing and attacking him, claiming to represent the voice either of reason or of the ancestral traditions. He was faced with what he called Satanic opposition from his own followers, even from his own chosen right-hand man. He spoke of having 'a baptism to be baptised with.' As he came to the end, he said to his followers, 'You are those who have continued with me in my trials, my testings.'

Finally, in Gethsemane, Jesus shrank from drinking the cup held out to him. But he turned that shrinking into agonised prayer, until finally he stretched out his hands, in obedience, to take the poisoned chalice. 'Behold, the handmaid of the Lord' – and, now, behold her son. This is what obedience looks like when it stares evil in the face.

Gethsemane suggests the deepest meanings of the prayer: 'Do not let us be led into the Testing, but deliver us from Evil.' Again and again Jesus says to his followers: Watch and pray, that you may not enter into Temptation. Now it would be absurd to suppose, at that moment of all moments, that Jesus was telling his followers to say their prayers in case they might be tempted to commit some trivial personal sin. No. Jesus has seen that the moment all his life has pointed towards – the moment all Israel's history has been driving towards – is rushing upon him. The word 'temptation' here means 'testing' or 'tribulation'. The great tribulation, the birthpangs of the new age, the moment of horror and deep darkness, is coming swiftly towards him. And in his own moment of agony he fears, with good reason, that the whirlpool of evil which is to engulf him will suck down his close followers as well. Jesus knows that he must go, solo and unaided, into the whirlpool, so that it may exhaust its force on him and let the rest of the world go free. And his followers must therefore pray: Let us not be brought into the Testing, into the great Tribulation; Deliver us from Evil.

We therefore have to come to grips with the fact that Jesus gave this prayer to his disciples, but that when he prayed it himself *the answer was 'No'*. He put it together with an earlier part of the Lord's Prayer ('Thy will be done'). When he held the two side by side, he found that God's will involved him in a unique vocation. He would be the one who *was* led to the Testing, who was *not* delivered from Evil.

Here, of course, we are at the brink of the great mystery: we only celebrate the Annunciation, along with Christmas itself, because this was where it all led. After all, lots of other Jewish girls hoped they would give birth to the Messiah; and even Mary's dream had to be dashed to smithereens in order that it might come true. Jesus was not called to be the sort of Messiah his Mother and her contemporaries had supposed. As Albert Schweitzer once put it, Jesus was called to throw himself on the wheel of world history, so that, even though it crushed him, it might start to turn in the opposite direction.

This vocation is unique to Jesus: where he goes, the rest of us cannot follow. The rest of us are therefore commanded to pray that we may be delivered from the power of Evil. And we can pray that prayer with confidence precisely because Jesus has met that power and has defeated it once and for all.

What, then, is evil, and how are we delivered from it? This question faces us, as that of guilt did in the last chapter, with three possible wrong answers.

The first answer is the head-in-the-sand approach. You can pretend that evil doesn't really exist, or that, if it does, it doesn't really matter. Yes, we say, people do silly things sometimes, but if we all try a little harder it'll work out all right. That's about as much use as saying, when the house is on fire, that yes, it is getting a little warm, but if we all take off a layer of clothing and drink more iced water things will be just fine.

The second answer, the mirror-image of the first, is to wallow in evil, and to see it all over the place. Once you realise that there is such a thing as radical evil, and that it's much more powerful than you are, you can either become evil yourself or become paranoid, seeing demons behind every bush. Either way, you are giving in – indeed, caving in, allowing evil to dominate you.

The third answer is that of self-righteousness. 'Lord, I thank thee that I am not as other people.' Yes, we say, evil is out there all right; but we are the righteous ones, the holy ones, called to leap on our white chargers and ride off to do battle with it. But what if self-righteous battles are themselves another manifestation of evil?

At the risk of caricature, you could say that, in Jesus' day, the first approach (minimising evil) was that of the Sadducees; the second (wallowing in the fact of evil) was that of the Essenes; and the third (the zealous fight against evil) was that of the Pharisees. Jesus adopts none of them, and he doesn't want his followers to, either. His way is to recognize the reality and power of evil, and to confront it with the reality and power of the kingdom-announcement. The result is Gethsemane and Calvary. His way for his followers is that they, too, recognize evil for what it is, and that they learn to pray, Deliver Us From Evil. To omit the petitions about 'testing' and 'evil' off the end of the prayer would indicate the first wrong route; to make them the only significant part of the prayer would be the second wrong route; to see yourself as the answer to the prayer, as the people through whose virtue the world will be delivered from evil, would be the third.

This prayer, in its setting within the whole Lord's Prayer, keeps the proper balance. Jesus intends his followers to recognize not only the reality of evil but the reality of his victory over it. We need to examine both sides of this balance.

Evil is real and powerful. It is not only 'out there', in other people, but it is present and active within each of us. What is more, 'evil' is more than the sum total of all evil impulses and actions. When human beings worship that which is not God, they give authority to forces of destruction and malevolence; and those forces gain a power, collectively, that has, down the centuries of Christian experience, caused wise people to personify it, to give it the name of Satan, the Accuser. 'The Satan', 'the Evil One', is not equal and opposite to God; but 'he', or 'it', is a potent force, opposed to God's good creation, and particularly to the human beings whom God wishes to put in authority over his world. If all this were not so, the final petition in the Lord's Prayer would be an unnecessary anti-climax.

But Jesus' victory over evil is also real and powerful. It, too, is not only 'out there', a fact of history two thousand years ago, but it is available here and now for each of us. Where human beings turn from idolatry and worship the God they see revealed on Calvary, they are turning from darkness to light, from the Strong Man to the one who has bound the Strong Man. To pray 'deliver us from evil', or 'from the evil one', is to inhale the victory of the cross, and thereby to hold the line for another moment, another hour, another day, against the forces of destruction within ourselves and the world.

You see, the only reason to shrink from a serious and radical analysis of evil would be if we were to forget that in the cross God has seriously and radically dealt with it. We are instinctively afraid of facing the evil that still lurks within us; we are, perhaps, also afraid of the humiliation involved in grasping God's solution to it. Our fear is natural. We are called to share in Mary's pain, the pain of being *theotokoi*, bearers of God's hopes and fears, focal points of the world's hopes and fears. But, fearful or not, this is the route we are called to take.

Let's get more specific. What might it mean for us to use this double clause of the Lord's Prayer as a way of breathing in this part of Jesus' agenda and vocation, and turning it into flesh and blood once more in and through our own life and work?

It means, first of all, signing on for a struggle and a battle. If Jesus, straight after his baptism, had to go out into the desert to face the whispering and mocking and wheedling and beguiling voices inside his own head, which he came to recognise as the voice of the enemy, why should we suppose we will be spared something of the same? 'My child', says the wise old Jewish writer Ben-Sira (2.1), 'If you come to serve the Lord, prepare yourself for testing.' The point about Christian faith and commitment is that you hold the faith, and stick to the commitment, in the teeth of apparent obstacles and enticements.

To say 'lead us not into temptation' does not, of course, mean that God himself causes people to be tempted. It has, rather, three levels of meaning. First, it means 'let us escape the great tribulation, the great testing, that is coming on all the world.' Finally, it means 'do not let us be led into temptation that we will be unable to bear' (compare 1 Corinthians 10.12–13). Finally, it means 'Enable us to pass safely through the testing of our faith'. Enable us, in other words, to hear the words of Annunciation and, though trembling, to say: Behold, the handmaid of the Lord. Thy will be done; deliver us from evil. We are thus to become people in whose lives the joy and pain of the whole world meet together once more, so that God's new world may at length come to birth.

This will mean different things for each of us, as we each grapple with our own testing and temptation. But, as we do so, we are caught up into something bigger than ourselves. We are part of that great movement whereby the hopes and fears of all the years are brought together and addressed by the living God. And, as we hear that gentle and powerful address to our own hopes and fears, we are called to become, in our turn, the means whereby that same address goes out to the wider world. We are called to pray alongside Mary as she offers herself, her joy and her pain, for the salvation of the world; alongside the disciples as, muddled and sleepy, they struggle and fail to pray with Jesus; above all, alongside Jesus himself, as he weeps in Gethsemane and staggers on to Calvary.

And, as we do so, we are called to look out on the world from that viewpoint and to pray, to pray earnestly, *Do not let us be led to the Test! Deliver us from Evil!* This is part of the prayer for the Kingdom:

it is the prayer that the forces of destruction, of dehumanization, of anti-creation, of anti-redemption, may be bound and gagged, and that God's good world may escape from being sucked down into their morass. It is our responsibility, as we pray this prayer, to hold God's precious and precarious world before our gaze, to sum up its often inarticulate cries for help, for rescue, for deliverance. Deliver us from the horror of war! Deliver us from human folly and the appalling accidents it can produce! Let us not become a society of rich fortresses and cardboard cities! Let us not be engulfed by social violence, or by self-righteous reaction! Save us from arrogance and pride and the awful things they make people do! Save us – from ourselves. . . and Deliver us from the Evil One.

And you can't pray these prayers from a safe distance. You can only pray them when you are saying Yes to God's Kingdom coming to birth within you, as Mary was called to do; when you are saying Yes to the call to follow Jesus to Gethsemane, even when you don't understand why; when you are saying Yes to the vocation to go to the place of pain, to share it in the name of Jesus, and to hold that pain prayerfully in the presence of the God who wept in Gethsemane and died on Calvary. Paul speaks, in a dramatic and daring passage (Colossians 1.24), of 'completing in my flesh that which is lacking in the afflictions of Christ'; and, in one of his greatest pieces of writing and of theology (Romans 8.18–27), he explains prayer in terms of the Spirit groaning within the Church as the Church groans within the World. The call to pray this clause of the prayer is therefore the call to be Annunciation-people; Gethsemane-people; and, yes, Calvary-people. We are called to live and pray at the place where the world is in pain, so that the hopes and fears, the joy and the pain of the whole world may become, by the Spirit and in our own experience, the hope and fear, the joy and pain of God.

By giving us this prayer, then, Jesus invites us to walk ahead into the darkness and discover that it, too, belongs to God. But, once we have entered the dark night, the fact that we have done so with the Lord's Prayer on our lips means that, when the darkness breaks it will be (not mere good cheer, but) glory itself that wakes: wakes with the human cry of a small baby, blinking up at his Mother in the sudden light, and seeing in her face, and reading in her heart, the hope and promise that God will triumph over fear, will deliver us from evil, and will bring in his Kingdom at last.

## CHAPTER SIX

# The Power and the Glory

'In those days,' says Luke, 'there went out a decree from the Emperor Augustus that all the world should be registered.' These words have become so well known, through constant repetition in carol services, that we may perhaps be forgiven for not stopping to reflect on what Luke is trying to tell us, here and throughout his work. In one short paragraph (2.1–14) he moves from the great Emperor in Rome to the new King who was to rule the world. There is no question, for Luke, as to which one makes the angels sing. As we look at this story, which we know so well and yet so little, we may catch a glimpse of what we might mean when we say: Thine is the Kingdom, the Power and the Glory.

By the time Jesus was born, Augustus had already been monarch of all he surveyed for a quarter of a century. He was the King of kings, ruling a territory that stretched from Gibralter to Jerusalem, from Britain to the Black Sea. He had done what no-one had done for two hundred years before him had achieved: he had brought peace to the whole wider Roman world. Peace, I grant you, at a price: a price paid, in cash, by subjects in far-off lands, and, in less obvious ways, by those who mourned the old Republic. Power was now concentrated in the hands of one man, whose kingdom stretched from shore to shore. And, as Arnaldo Momigliano, one of the greatest of ancient historians, once put it, '[Augustus] gave peace, as long as it was consistent with the interests of the Empire and the myth of his own glory'. There you have it in a nutshell: the whole ambiguous structure of human empire, a kingdom of absolute power, bringing glory to the man at the top, and peace to those on whom his favour rested.

Yes, says Luke, and watch what happens now. This man, this king, this absolute monarch, lifts his little finger in Rome, and fifteen hundred miles away in an obscure province a young couple undertake a hazardous journey, resulting in the birth of a child in a little town that just happens to be the one mentioned in the ancient Hebrew prophecy about the coming of the Messiah. And it is at this birth that the angels sing of glory and peace. Which is the reality, and which the parody?

Here we have to pause again, because the passage from Micah 5, which Luke intends to awaken in our minds, is so well known and so little attended to. 'But you, Bethlehem of Ephrathah, little among the clans of Judah – from you shall come forth the one who is to rule in Israel' (Micah 5.2). The passage is regularly cut off, when read in public, a verse or two early. Verse 4 launches a project that ought to make Augustus anxious: 'He [that is, the coming King] shall stand and feed his flock in the strength of YHWH, in the majesty of the name of YHWH his God; and they shall live secure, for now he shall be great to the ends of the earth.' But the next verse goes on: 'And he shall be the man of peace.'

How is this peace to be secured? The following verses describe how this coming King, born in Bethlehem of Judea, will rescue his people from the hand of the foreign emperors. In Micah's day, this was Assyria; but Luke's readers would have had no difficulty in transferring the meaning to Rome, and Luke would have hoped that subsequent generations would have been equally adept at contemporary applications. Herod was worried by what the Wise Men told him. If someone had told Augustus what the angels had said to the shepherds, he'd have been worried too.

Suddenly, as we watch what Luke is doing, the scene ceases to be a romantic pastoral idyll, with the rustic shepherds paying homage to the infant king. It becomes a fairly clear statement of two kingdoms, kingdoms that are destined to compete, kingdoms that offer radically different definitions of what peace and power and glory are all about.

Here is the old king in Rome, turning sixty in the year Jesus was born: he represents perhaps the best that pagan kingdoms can do. At least he knows that peace and stability are good things; unfortunately he has had to kill a lot of people to bring them about, and to kill a lot more, on a regular basis, to preserve them. Unfortunately, too, his real interest is in his own glory. Already, before his death, many of his subjects have begun to regard him as divine.

Here, by contrast, is the young king in Bethlehem, born with a price on his head. He represents the dangerous alternative, the possibility of a different empire, a different power, a different glory, a different peace. The two systems stand over against one another. Augustus' empire is like a well-lit room at night. The lamps are arranged beautifully; they shed pretty patterns; but they haven't defeated the darkness outside. Jesus' kingdom is like the morning star rising, signalling that it's time to blow out the candles, to throw open the curtains, and to welcome the new day that is dawning. Glory to God in the highest – and peace among those with whom he is pleased!

It is this double vision of reality that we invoke every time we conclude the Lord's Prayer with the words 'For thine is the kingdom, the power and the glory, for ever and ever.' This concluding doxology doesn't appear in the best manuscripts of either Matthew or Luke, and it is only comparatively recently, in the last few centuries, that it has been restored to the liturgy of the Western church. But it was already well established within a century or so of Jesus' day; and it is actually inconceivable, within the Jewish praying styles of his day, that Jesus would have intended the prayer to stop simply with 'deliver us from evil'. Something like this must have been intended from the beginning. In any case, it chimes in exactly with the message of the prayer as a whole: God's kingdom, God's power, and God's glory are what it's all about. It is the prayer that the alternative vision of reality may become, not just a vision, but reality. It is the prayer that the baby in Bethlehem may be the reality of which Augustus is the parody.

The prayer thus encapsulates, once more, the whole life and work of Jesus. John sums it up in his own way: the Word became flesh, and dwelt among us; and we beheld his glory, glory as of the only-begotten of the Father, full of grace and truth. That, please note, is a careful *redefinition* of 'glory'. When you look at the Word become flesh, you don't see the sort of glory that Augustus Caesar and his like work for. You see the glory that is the family likeness of God himself. Caesar's glory is full of brute force and deep ambiguity. God's glory – Jesus' glory – is full of grace and truth. The royal babe in the cowshed overturns all that human empire stands for.

You see the two empires squared off against each other towards the end of John's gospel, when Pilate confronts Jesus with two questions: don't you know that I have the power to have you killed? And – what is truth? That is the language of kingdom, power and glory that the world knows. Notice how the two halves support each other. In order to be able to say, 'Support my kingdom or I'll kill you', pagan empire needs to say that there's no such thing as truth. And if someone not only tells the truth but lives the truth, pagan empire has no alternative but to kill them. Jesus responds by quietly reminding Pilate that all power comes from on high, and by getting on with the job of *being* the truth – living out truly the love of God for the salvation of the world. Luke's message of the baby in the manger stands over against even the best pagan empires, inviting us to contemplate the radical and total redefinition of truth, of peace, and above all of kingdom, power and glory.

This final clause in the Lord's Prayer points us to two aspects of Jesus' life and work which we must put in place if we are not to leave the present little book as a headless torso. We have seen what it meant for Jesus to call God 'Father'; we have seen the doubly revolutionary meaning of his prayer for the Kingdom, the rich provision of daily bread and the astonishment of forgiveness. We have seen Jesus go to the place of darkness, to confront and defeat evil on its own turf. But now, as we put the whole package together, what can we say about Jesus himself?

The clue to this question is found in some more of the strange stories Jesus told. Jesus repeatedly told stories about a master, a king or a father going away and coming back again. He would return at last, to see what his servants had been up to in his absence. (We looked at this theme briefly in the chapter on the Kingdom.) From quite early on, the church read these stories in terms of Jesus' own second coming. Jesus had gone away in the Ascension, and would return on

the last day as Saviour and Judge. But it seems clear
to me that Jesus himself did not intend that meaning,
at least as the basic one. His hearers were, after all,
eagerly awaiting the Kingdom of God; and one part
of that package, ever since Isaiah's Advent message,
was the theme of YHWH's return to Zion. Israel's
God had abandoned his sinful people to their fate of
exile; but he would return at last, to be king over all
the earth. This is the kingdom-and-power-and-glory
theme, scored for full brass and organ: the glory of
the Lord shall be revealed, and all flesh shall see it
together.

Jesus not only tells stories about this happening at
last; he behaves as if he thinks it is happening in and
through his own work. Exchange the full brass for
trembling woodwind. As Jesus told the great story, of
the nobleman returning to find out what his servants
had done in his absence, he was himself approaching
Jerusalem; and, with the warnings of that parable still
ringing in his followers' ears, he rode over the Mount
of Olives on a donkey and wept over the city. If only
you had known, he said through his tears, the things
that make for peace; but now they are hidden from
your eyes. Your enemies, the Romans, will come and
destroy you, because you did not know the time of
God's visitation.

So saying, Jesus rode into the city and proceeded to act out a parable of judgment upon the Temple. This is what Advent looks like in flesh and blood: the Lord whom ye seek shall suddenly come to his Temple; but who may abide the day of his coming? Jesus had come as the Bethlehem Jesus, the Prince of Peace; and Jerusalem had refused his way of peace, opting instead for the way of the sword, which, as Jesus himself said to Peter, could have only one result. Jesus as an adult acted out the message the angels had sung at his birth; but, when he came to his own, his own received him not. Luke tells us in his way what John tells us in his: Jesus was not just the spokesman for Israel's God; he was the very word of God, Israel's God in person, acting out unequivocally the return of YHWH to Zion.

Once again, then, there went out a decree from Caesar, which had a profound effect fifteen hundred miles away: rebel kings get crucified. If you let this man go, said the chief priests to Pilate, you are not Caesar's friend. This, then, was what it would look like when the ancient promises were fulfilled, when the glory of the Lord would be revealed for all flesh to see together: a young Jew, riding over the Mount of Olives in tears, driving the traders out of the Temple, and dying at the behest of Caesar's kingdom.

And once again, Luke intends us to realise, the angels are singing that God is glorified, and that the way of peace has been achieved after all. This is the ultimate redefinition of the kingdom, the power and the glory. Caesar's plans for his own glory are turned by God into the establishment of the true Kingdom.

How, then, are we to take this final clause of the Lord's Prayer, and to use it to breathe in Jesus' message, his agenda, his very life, and to make it our own? Three things by way of conclusion.

First, this is the prayer of mission and commission. If Jesus is the true King of all the world, whose kingdom redefines power and glory so that they are now seen in the manger, on the cross, and in the garden, then to pray this prayer is to pray that this kingdom, this power and this glory may be seen in all the world. It is not enough, though it is the essential starting-point, that we submit in our own lives to God's alternative kingdom-vision; we must pray and work for the vision to come in reality, with the rulers of this world being confronted with the claims of their rightful king.

We cannot, then, pray this prayer and acquiesce in the power and glory of Caesar's kingdom. Augustus would have known quite well what was going on if he'd heard anyone praying this prayer, and he would have trembled on his throne. If the church isn't prepared to subvert the kingdoms of the world with the kingdom of God, the only honest thing would be to give up praying this prayer altogether, especially its final doxology.

Second, this is the prayer of incarnation and empowerment. Jesus lived the Kingdom because he *was* the rightful king. But we, who take upon ourselves the holy boldness to join him in calling God 'Abba, Father', believe that we have been anointed with Jesus' Spirit; 'anointing', of course, being part of what 'Messiah' means. The church that prays this prayer does so as the new royal family – which lives by, and only by, that radical redefinition of kingship, of royalty, which we discover in the manger and on the cross. Just as Jesus was asked by what authority he was acting, and answered by referring back to his anointing, the church should be active within the world as the people of the true King, as the Christ-people, and should be prepared to justify that action by appealing to her royal, anointed status. To pray this prayer is therefore to invoke the power of the Spirit of Jesus, as we work for the glory of God in his anointed son.

Thirdly, this is the prayer of confidence and commitment. It is the prayer that rounds off and seals off all the others. It is because God is King, and has become King in Jesus, that we can pray the rest of the prayer with confidence. The gospels contain a good many remarkable promises about what happens when people pray in the name of Jesus. Those who take those promises seriously often report that, in William Temple's famous words, 'When I pray, coincidences happen; when I stop praying, the coincidences stop happening'.

Such prayer, in the name of Jesus, isn't magic. Sometimes people try to use it as such. Others, reacting against such nonsense, back off from the boldness and confidence that should characterize the prayer of children to their Father. Rather, to pray in Jesus' name is to invoke the name of the Stronger than the Strong; it is to appeal to the one through whom the creator of the world has become king, has taken the power of the world and has defeated it with the power of the cross, has confronted the glory of the world and has outshone it with the glory of the cross. When people in Jesus' world backed up a request with the Emperor's name, people jumped to attention. How much more, when we pray in the name of the true King of kings?

Of course, when we pray in the name of Jesus, we find, again and again, that what we want to pray for subtly changes as we focus on Jesus himself. Part of the game is the readiness, in great things and small, to put our plans and hopes on hold and let God remake them as we gaze upon him, revealed in the inglorious glory of the manger, in the powerless power of the cross. But when we allow that to happen, bit by bit, and then come with holy boldness into the presence of our Father, we discover that he really does have, prepared for those who love him, such good things as pass human understanding. Charles Wesley caught the mood of the end of the Lord's Prayer, celebrating Jesus' first coming and eagerly awaiting his final coming to fulfil all things, when he wrote:

Yea, Amen! Let all adore thee,
High on thine eternal throne;
Saviour, take the power and glory:
Claim the Kingdom for thine own:
O come quickly!
Alleluia! Come, Lord, Come!